VOCABIRDS

VOCABULARY WORKBOOK

GRADE 3

Spell-o-Fun

Help the Vocabird match the pictures to their names.

bagpipes

appliances

groundnuts

bookmark

butterfly

parachute

grasshopper

Who Let The Vowels Out?

It seems like the vowels have found a way to get out of words! Help the Vocabird choose the correct vowel keys to complete the words.

n _ g h t d r _ s s

h _ r i z _ n t _ l

m _ c r _ s c _ p _

s c h _ _ l m _ t _

b _ s k _ t b _ l l

p _ s s _ n g _ r

b _ d c _ v _ r _ n g

f _ n g _ r p r _ n t

WORD SCRAMBLE

Look at the pictures and unscramble the words to spell them correctly.

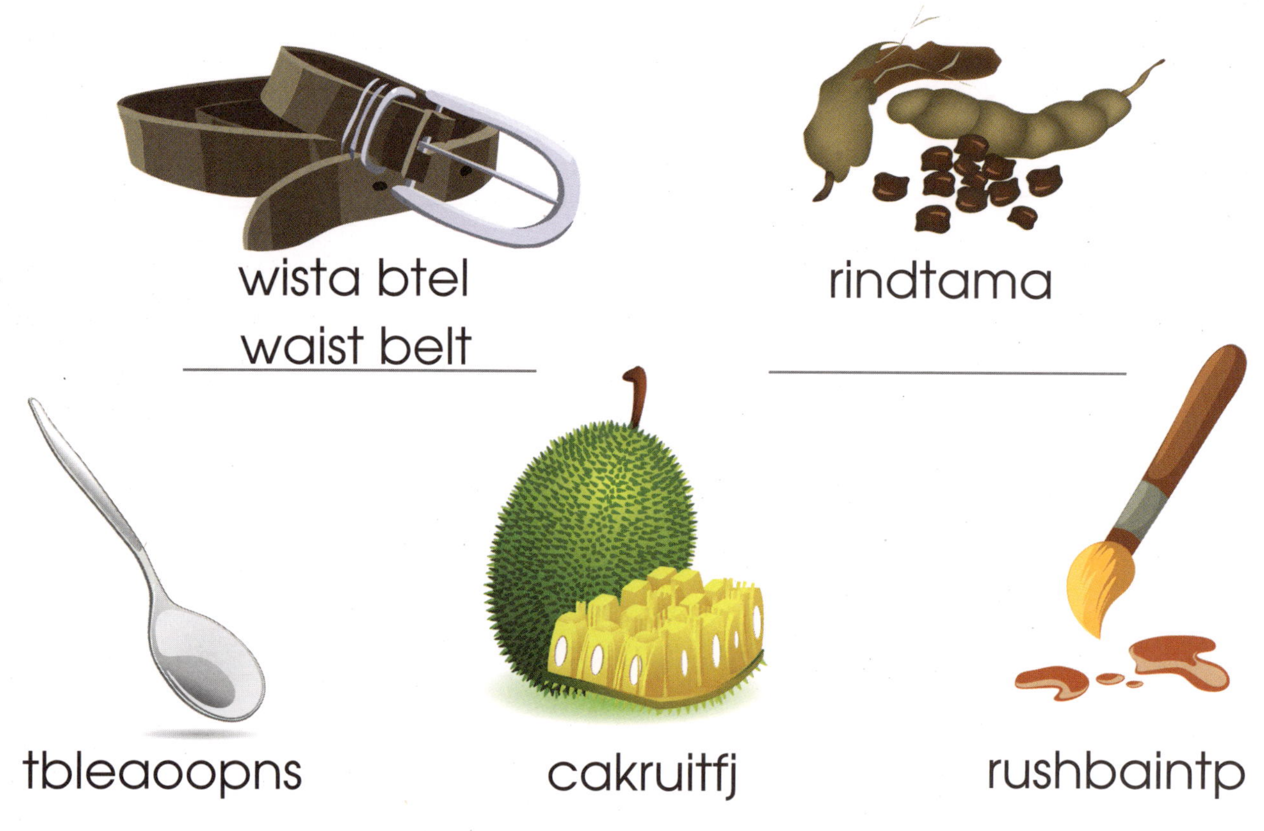

wista btel

waist belt

rindtama

____

tbleaoopns

____

cakruitfj

____

rushbaintp

____

llaumbres

____

silabota

____

Tri-spotting

Help the Vocabird circle the trigraphs in the words given below.

Voca tip: Trigraphs are groups of three letters in a word which make the same sound. For example: eau, igh, sch, tch, scr, squ, spr, shr, ure, air, eau, thr, spl, dge, etc.

TRI-FILLER

Fill in the blanks with the correct trigraph to name the pictures.

s q u irrel

___ ___ ___ out

___ ___ ___ one

b ___ ___ ___

___ ___ ___ ool

___ ___ ___ ew

MAGIC LETTER "E"

Add the letter "e" and make new words.

Voca tip: When we add an "e" to a word, it changes the sound of the other vowel in the word. For example: sit - site

Diphthongs

Help the Vocabird write words on each house using the diphthong written above.

Voca tip: Diphthong is one sound created by two vowels in a word.

WORD HUNT

Spot and circle these names in the grid below.

grasshopper | cocoon | ostrich
kangaroo | dragonfly | cricket

q	s	g	r	e	e	n	e	w	g	x
k	a	n	g	a	r	o	o	t	r	c
j	a	j	o	j	c	a	l	h	a	r
z	a	b	s	f	o	h	a	a	s	o
v	f	g	t	d	c	l	d	l	s	c
s	p	a	r	r	o	w	y	l	h	o
g	s	h	i	a	o	m	b	k	o	d
h	k	d	c	e	n	z	u	m	p	i
j	r	t	h	d	x	v	g	e	p	l
d	r	a	g	o	n	f	l	y	e	e
c	r	i	c	k	e	t	i	q	r	d

CLUB "O" CLOCK

Look at the pictures and club their names to create the name of a new animal.

+ = jellyfish

+ = ____________

+ = ____________

+ = ____________

Animals From the Past

Unscramble the words in the green eggs using the clues given alongside. Write the correct answers in the yellow eggs.

I arrived in the British Isles at the end of the Ice Age 12,000 years ago.

I belong to the penguin family.

I am a close relative of the lion. I am European.

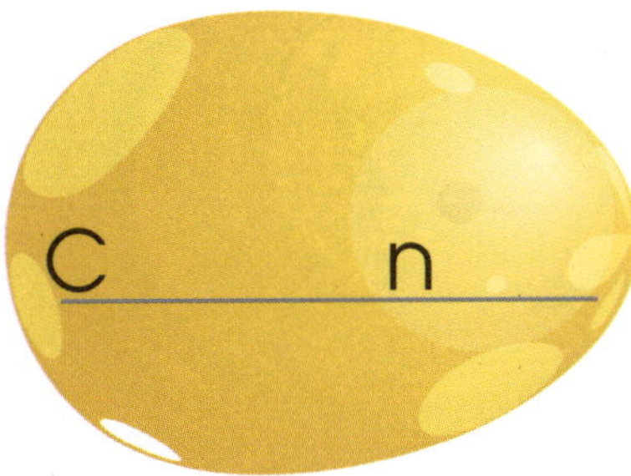

I was the largest marine animal after whales.

Unscramble the clues and help the Vocabird find the extinct animals in the crossword.

Across:

1) seaca
2) saurdino
3) dodo

Down:

4) dontoxo
5) donmasto
6) ggaqua

GETTING TO WORK

Match the names of the professionals to the correct pictures.

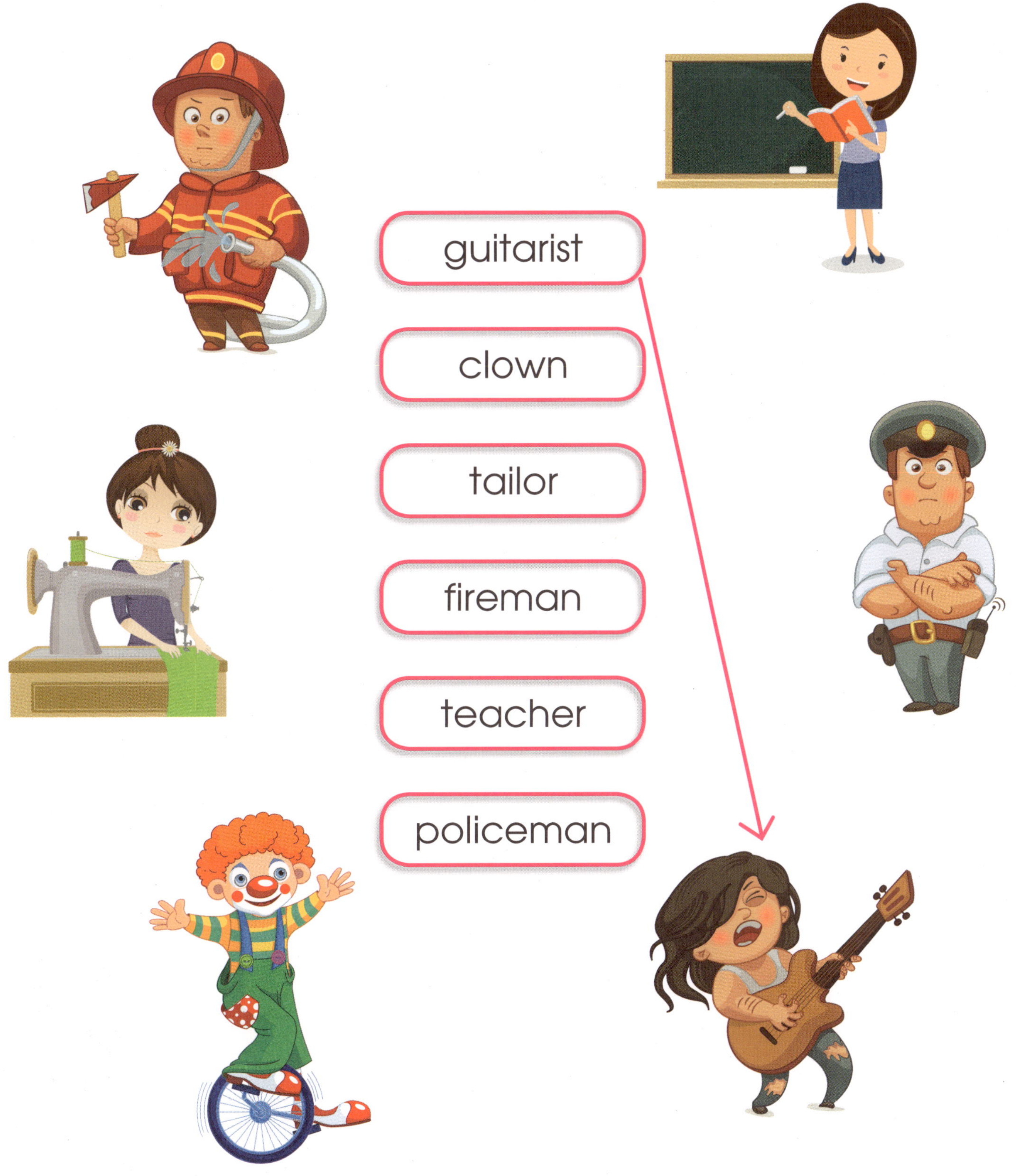

What's My Job?

This Vocabird is confused about his career. Help him sort his confusion by filling the blanks.

1) I work for a newspaper or a TV channel.
   I am a reporter.

2) I fight crime and arrest criminals.
   I am a ______________________.

3) I help you to learn at school.
   I am a ______________________.

4) I play a guitar.
   I am a ______________________.

5) I save people from the fire.
   I am a ______________________.

6) I earn a living by playing sports.
   I am a ______________________.

7) I prepare meals in a restaurant.
   I am a ______________________.

Dictionary Wise

Use the dictionary and help the Vocabird to circle the correct spelling.

Voca tip: You can start by looking at the first letter in the dictionary, then checking for the second letter and so on.

Speech Therapy

Help the Vocabird put the words in the correct baskets.

Voca tip: Do this exercise with the help of a dictionary.

funnel saturate wavelength

rustic marmalade mustard

beautiful clipboard youthful

tilt artificial handle

noun adjective verb

TECHNOWORLD

This Vocabird is hungry. To reach food, he has to select the words that are related to technology. Help him follow the correct path!

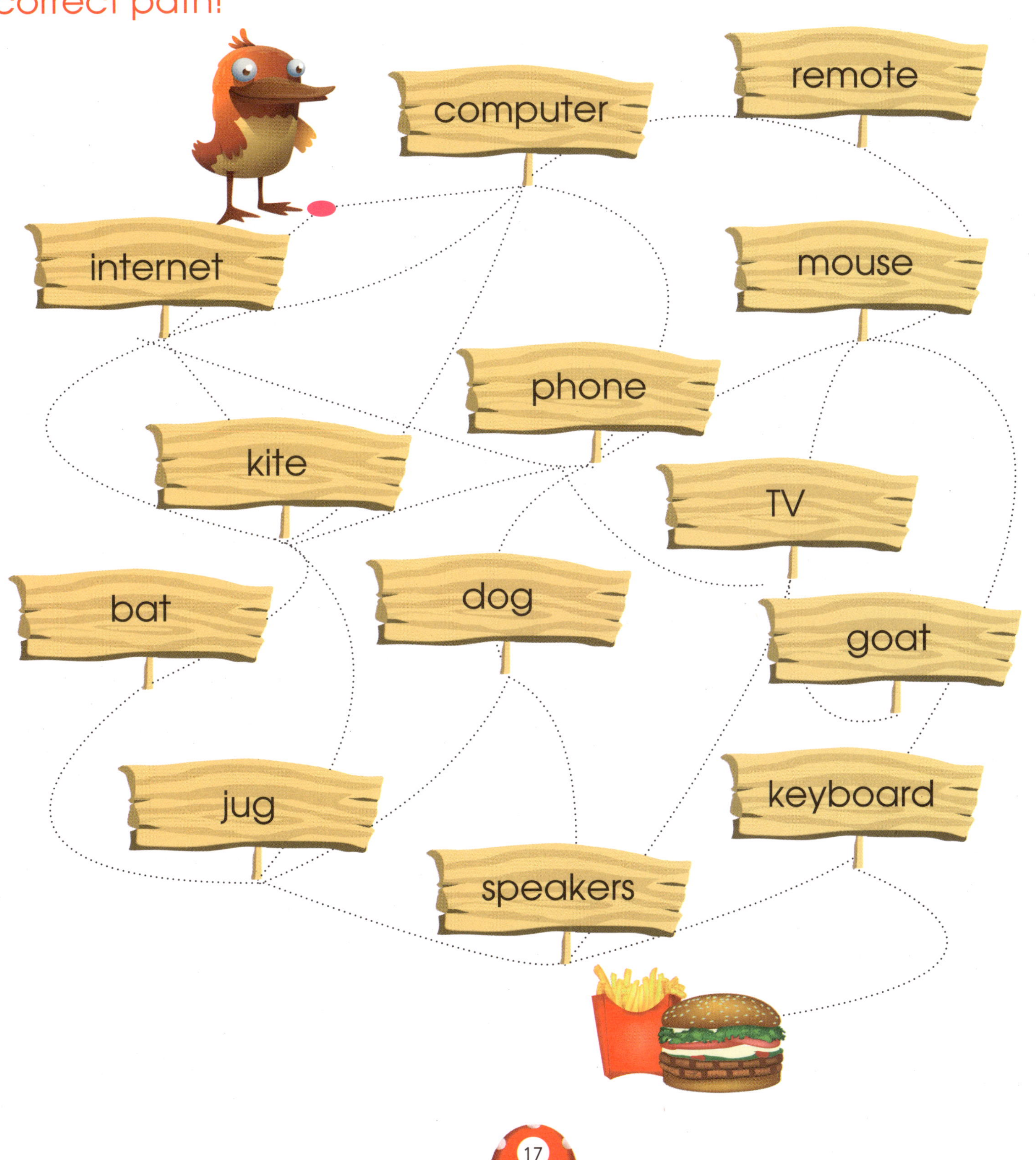

Work Woes

Unscramble the words and write the names of the devices shown in the picture.

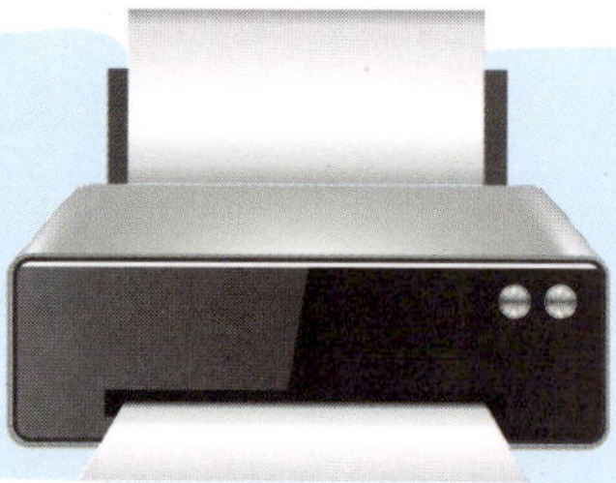

ipnerrt	printer
esarer	
unchepr	
koobslhef	
licpen	

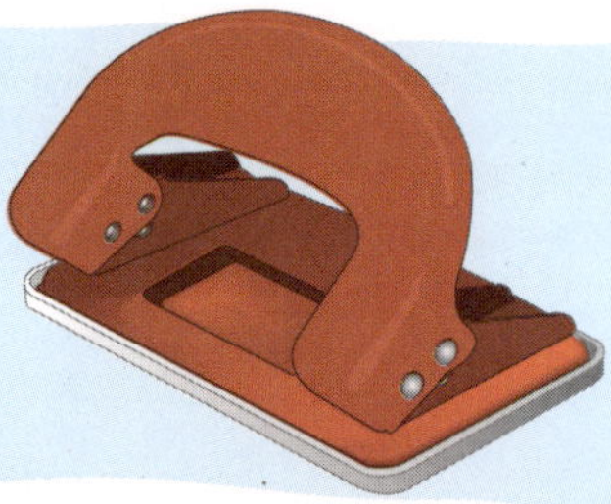

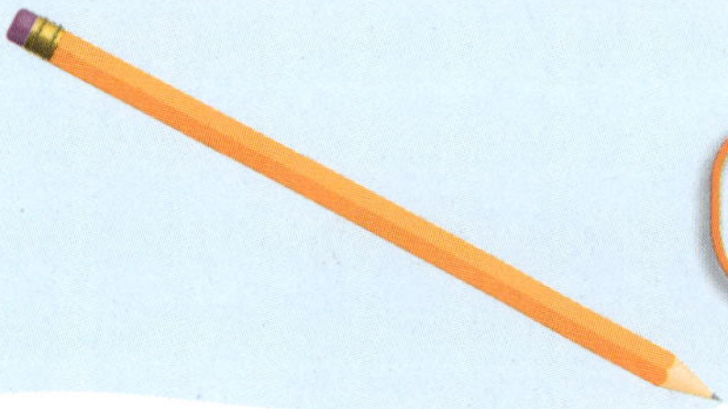

Work Woes

culatorcal

terupmoc

mpal

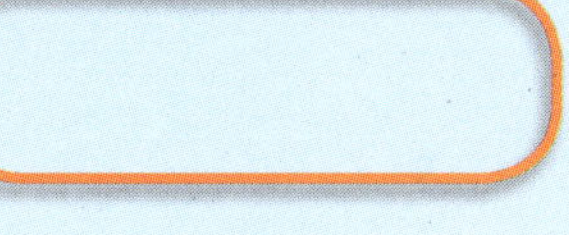

plersta

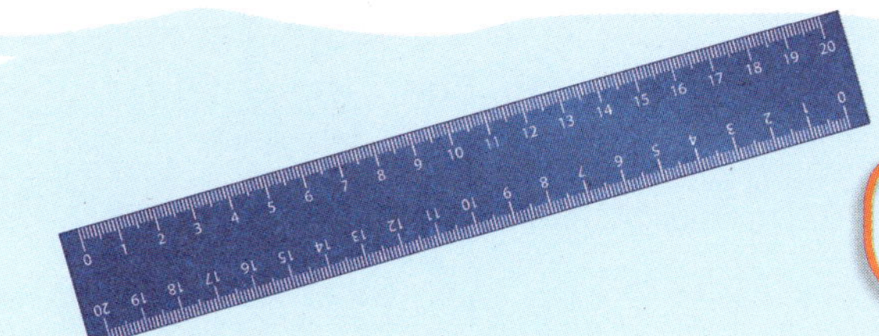

lerru

Lettery Woes

Look at the pictures and fill in the blanks with the correct letters for the Vocabird.

c<u>a</u>r

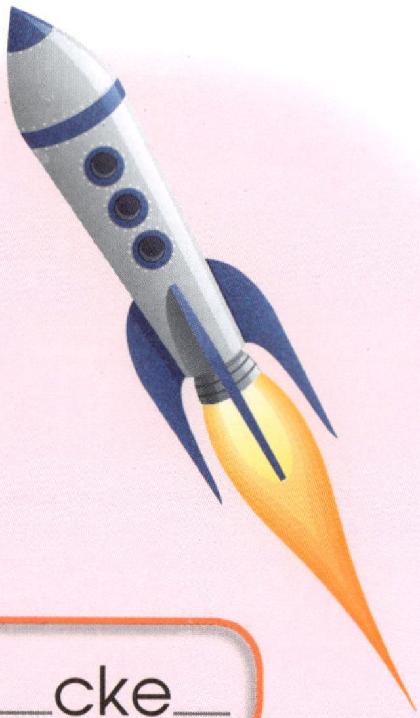

r_cke_

pri_ter

a_r c_ndi_ion_r

m_b_le p_on_

Amazing Antonyms

Spot and underline the antonyms in the sentences given below.

1) The teacher said yes but mom said no.

2) Ron was supposed to throw the ball and Shaun was supposed to catch it.

3) Instead of launching attacks, we decided to defend.

4) The arrival and departure of both the trains is almost at the same time.

5) It is very dark inside, even though it is bright outside.

6) Jack came first and John came last in the race.

7) I hate eating vegetables but love eating ice cream.

8) Please come soon as we need to go out afterwards.

Opposite Choices

Help the Vocabird fill in the blanks with the correct antonyms.

1) present X past

past	out	squeak

2) receive X ________

kite	give	small

3) walk X ________

fast	in	run

4) fast X ________

high	slow	low

5) pick X ________

wrong	yes	drop

6) alive X ________

dead	big	cat

7) cry X ________

jug	laugh	still

Syno-match

Help the Vocabird match the synonym eggs to the correct nests.

Perfect Pairs

Can you circle the synonym pairs for the Vocabird?

everyday few

tiny small

night day

thin sunny

giggle laugh

hurt safe

garbage trash

answer reply

finished done

WORDY MATH

Add the words below to make new compound words.

Voca tip: Compound words are made by joining two or more words.

for + ever	=	forever
down + stairs	=	
in + side	=	
up + scale	=	
milk + shake	=	
birth + day	=	
house + boat	=	
row + house	=	
tube + light	=	
door + way	=	

Word Partners

Help the Vocabird match the words from the boxes to their partners below.

with	basket	down	fire
after	any	eye	snow
hand	play	tooth	

ground	fall	brow
pour	noon	way
shake	out	man
	brush	ball

Kangaroo Words

Help the Vocabird circle baby words from the given kangaroo words.

Voca tip: Kangaroo words carry baby words in themselves.

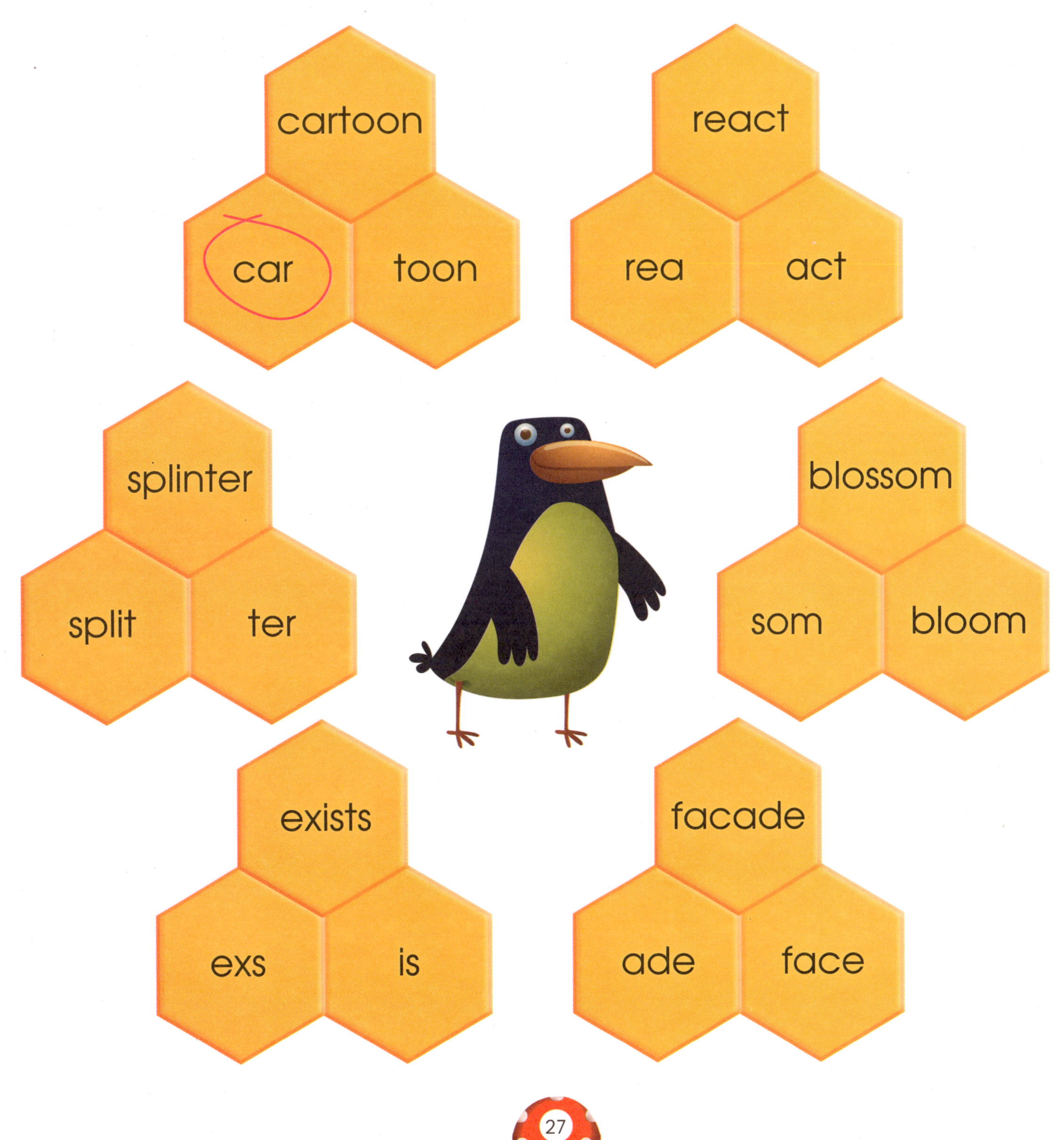

Wordsmithing

Help the Vocabird become a wordsmith by filling the blanks with baby words from the box.

story be use mark curt

east rain lush rim sack

beca<u>use</u>________ ________fall ________ain

f________ hi________ ________et

________at p________ p________er

Word Trekking

Help the Vocabird reach the top of the mountain by choosing nouns from the water and writing them on the rocks.

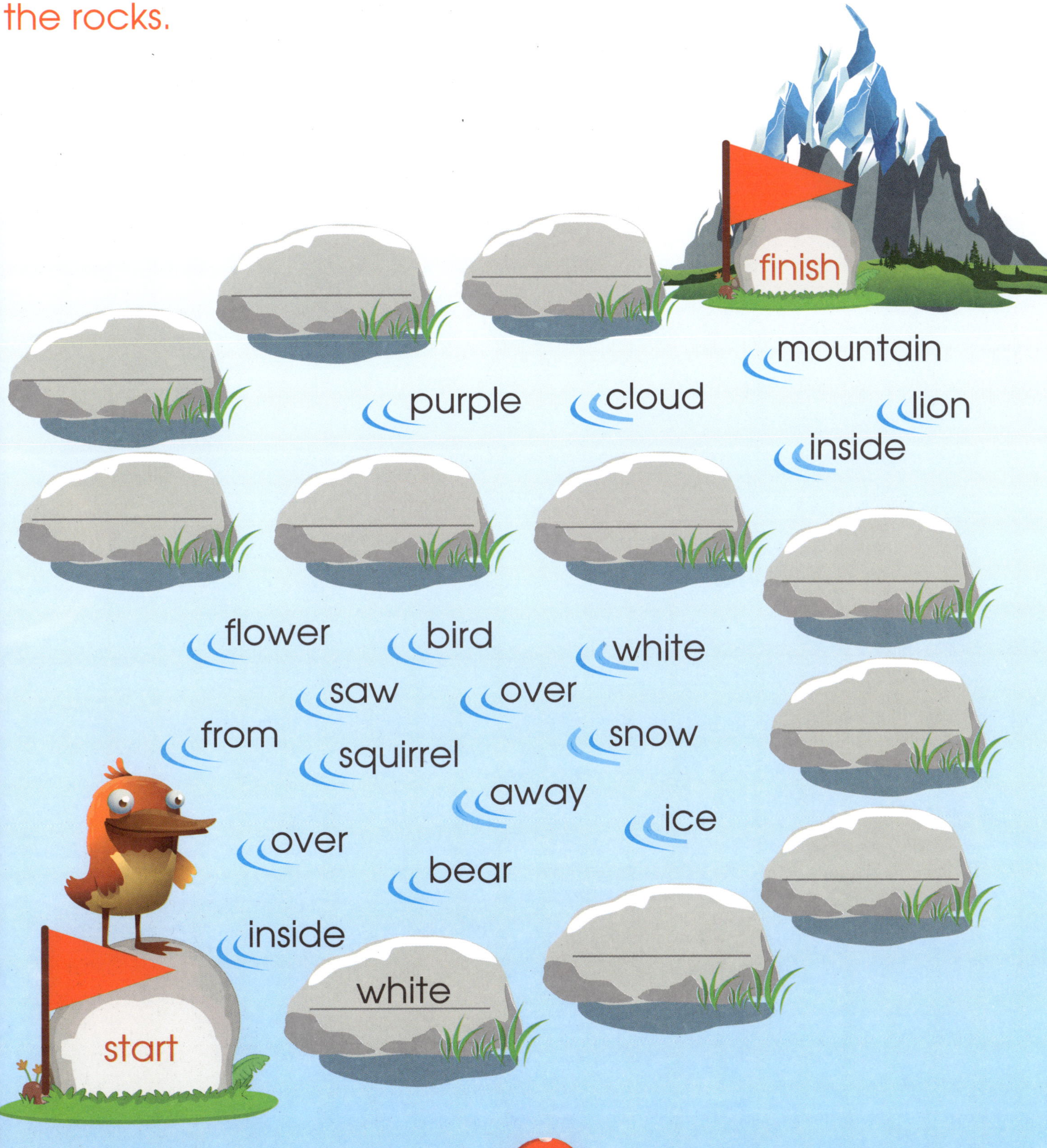

Homophone Mania

Help the Vocabird fill in the blanks with the correct homophones.

1) Have you read the story about the tortoise and the hare? (hair/hare)

2) __________ going to be freezing outside. (Its/It's)

3) I want to have the __________ sandwich by myself. (whole/hole)

4) I won the match by __________ points. (four/fore)

5) I would like __________ have a new dress for my birthday. (to/two)

6) Please make sure that __________ wearing formals for the interview. (you're/your)

7) I want to be __________ for her graduation ceremony. (there/their)

Answers

Page 2

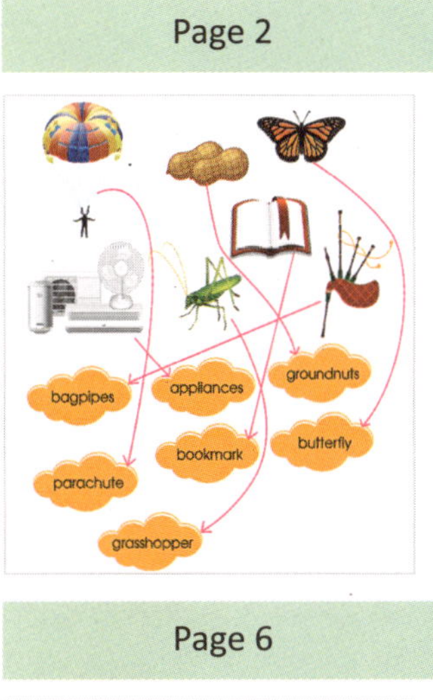

Page 3

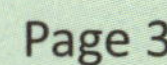

Page 4

Page 5

Page 6

Page 7

Page 8

ANSWERS WILL VARY

Page 9

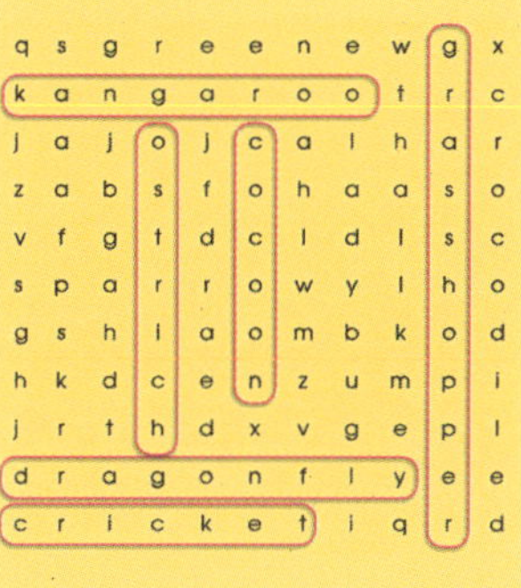

Page 10

Page 11

Page 12

Page 13

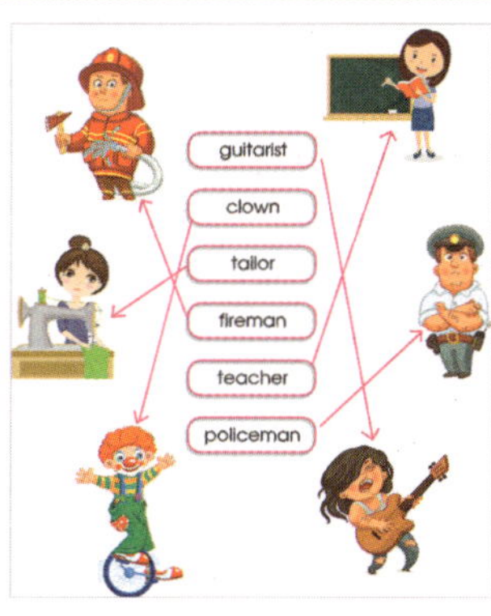

Page 14

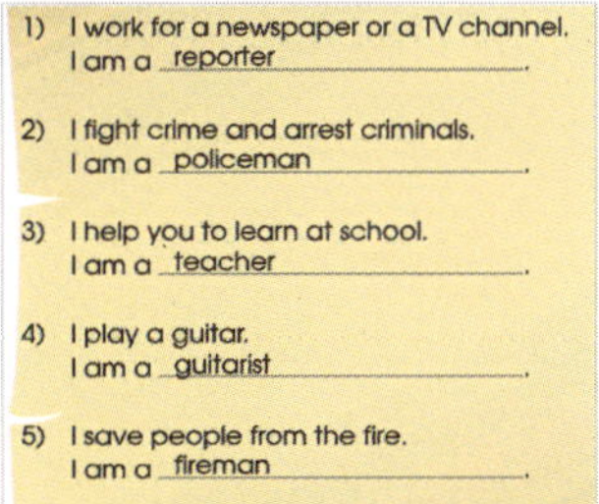

1) I work for a newspaper or a TV channel.
I am a reporter
2) I fight crime and arrest criminals.
I am a policeman
3) I help you to learn at school.
I am a teacher
4) I play a guitar.
I am a guitarist
5) I save people from the fire.
I am a fireman
6) I earn a living by playing sports.
I am a sportsman
7) I prepare meals in a restaurant.
I am a chef

Page 15

Page 16

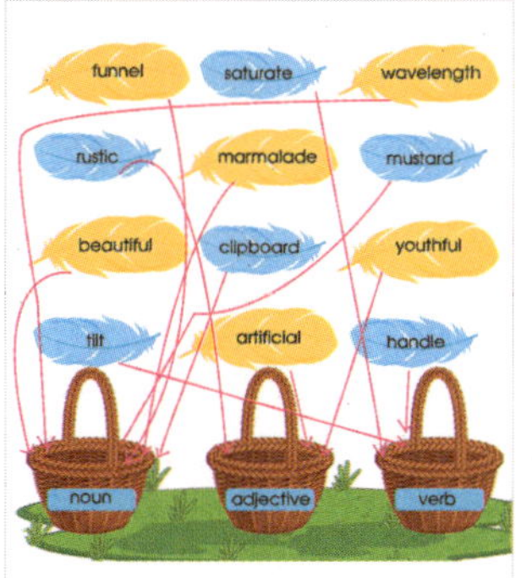

Page 17

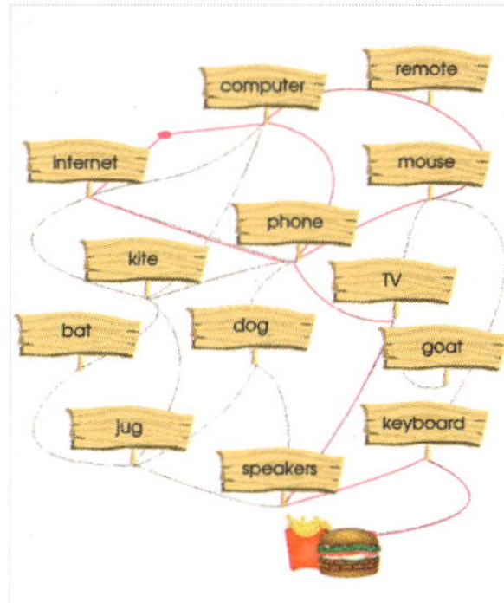

Answers

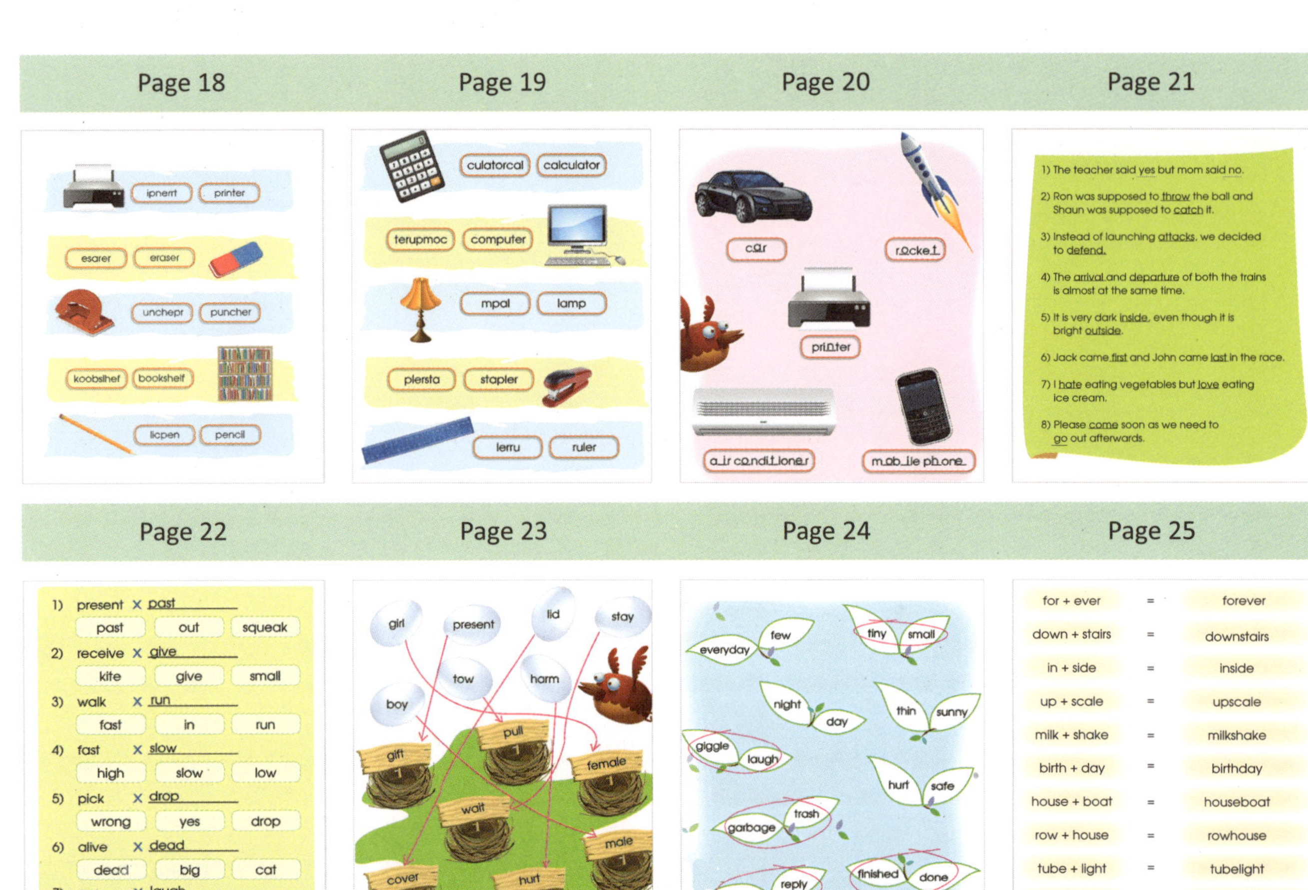

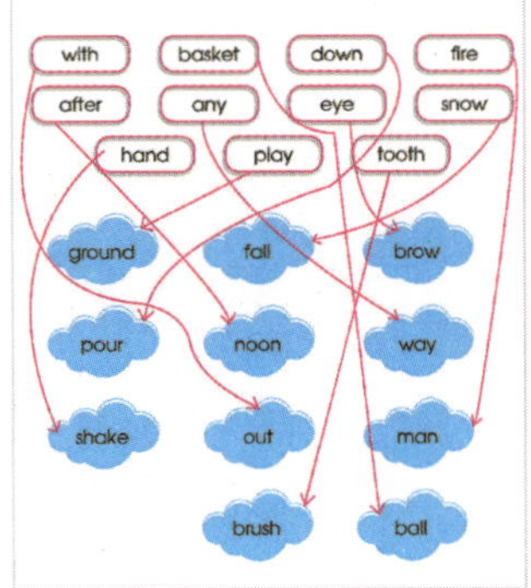

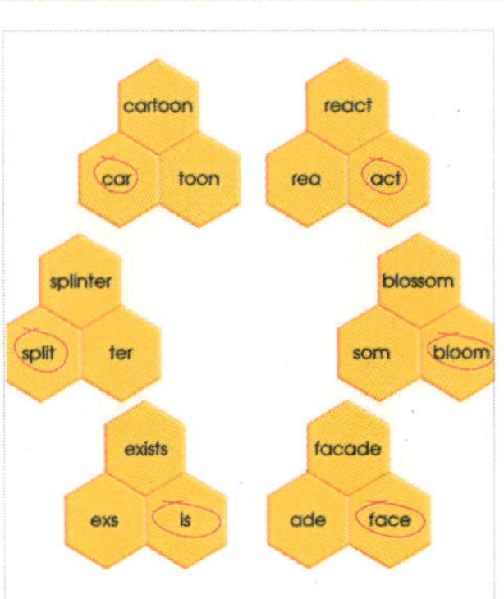

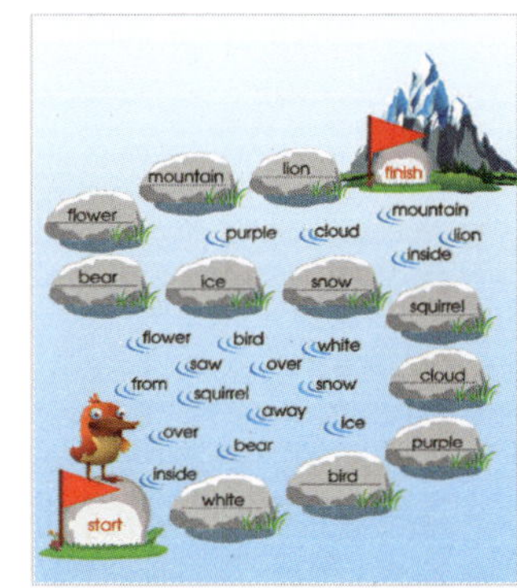

Page 30

1) Have you read the story about the tortoise and the hare? (hair/hare)
2) It's going to be freezing outside. (Its/It's)
3) I want to have the whole sandwich by myself. (whole/hole)
4) I won the match by four points. (four/fore)
5) I would like to have a new dress for my birthday. (to/two)
6) Please make sure that you're wearing formals for the interview. (you're/your)
7) I want to be there for her graduation ceremony. (there/their)

Anagrams

An anagram is a word or phrase made by rearranging the letters of another word or phrase.

Example: spot- pots, post, stop

Rearrange the letters in each word below and write an anagram in the space provided.

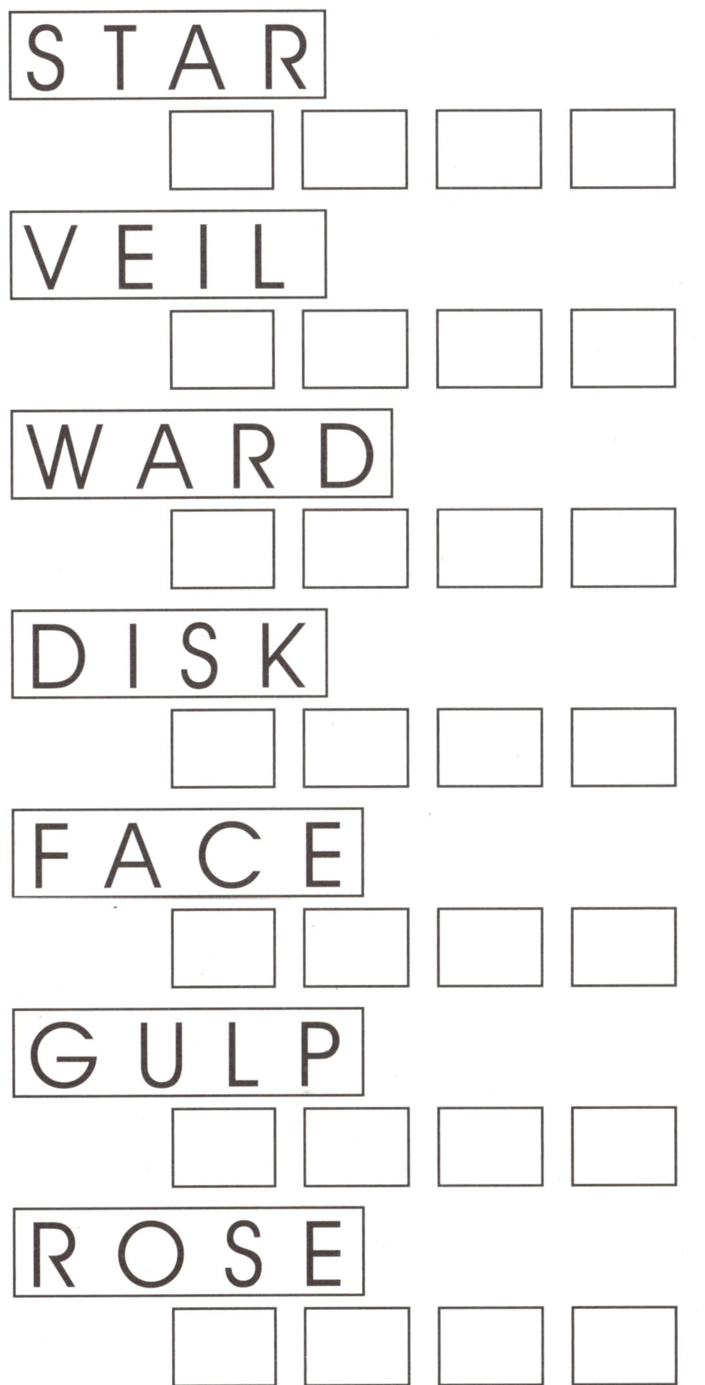

Rearrange the letters to form the surprise answer.

I G E H T   T A E

Root Words

A root word is the basic word that exists in a language. It has no added letters. We can add letters to root words to make other words and change their meaning.

example: play, give, jam

replay is not a root word as it has re + play in it

Look at the words on each cap. Colour the cap if the word is a root word.

Root Words

Identify the root word of the words in the word bank. Complete each sentence using the root words.

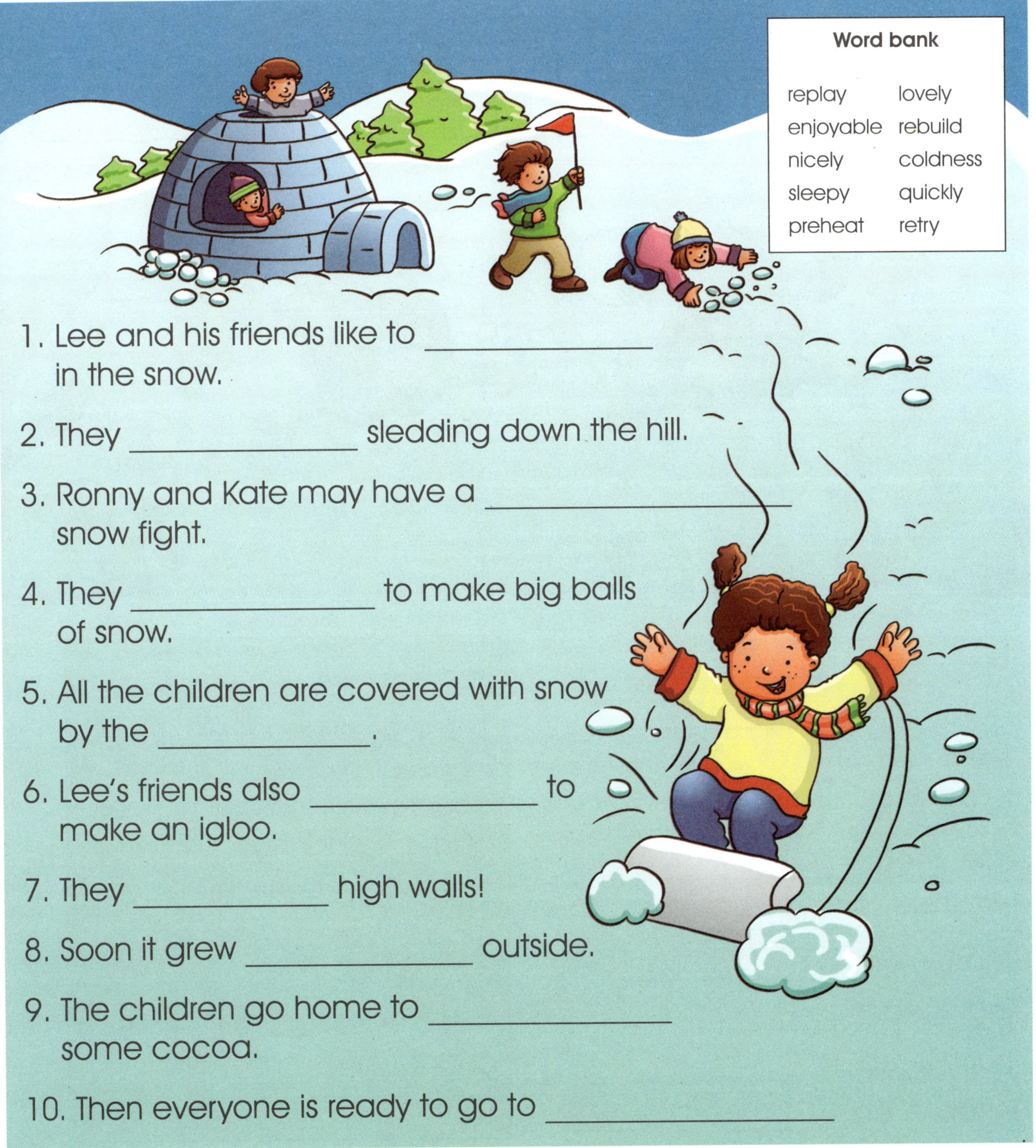

Word bank

replay	lovely
enjoyable	rebuild
nicely	coldness
sleepy	quickly
preheat	retry

1. Lee and his friends like to ______________ in the snow.
2. They ______________ sledding down the hill.
3. Ronny and Kate may have a ______________ snow fight.
4. They ______________ to make big balls of snow.
5. All the children are covered with snow by the ______________.
6. Lee's friends also ______________ to make an igloo.
7. They ______________ high walls!
8. Soon it grew ______________ outside.
9. The children go home to ______________ some cocoa.
10. Then everyone is ready to go to ______________

Inflectional Endings

Inflectional endings are letters added to the end of a word that change its meaning. **-s, -ed, -ing, -er, -est** are inflectional endings.

Example: play- plays, played, playing

Write each new word on the line. Follow the spelling rules.

1. dive + ed = ____________
2. carry + ed= ____________
3. talk + ed = ____________
4. wash + ed = ____________
5. skip + ed = ____________
6. try + ed = ____________
7. plan + ed = ____________
8. jog + ed = ____________
9. hurry + ed = ____________
10. hop + ed = ____________

Spelling rules

1. If a word ends with a short vowel and one consonant, double the consonant. Then add – *ed or –ing.*

2. If a word ends with *e*, drop the *e* and then add –*ed or –ing.*

3. If a word ends with *y*, change the y to *i*. Then add *–ed.*

Inflectional Endings

Read the words in the word bank.
Add –ed, -ing, or -s and then write the word in the correct group.

Word bank

flap	hope	plan
lift	fit	grab
cook	sting	drag
skip	jump	crawl
save	walk	melt

Add -s

Add -ed

Add -ing

Prefixes

A prefix is a word part added at the beginning of a base word to change the meaning of that word.

Example: re + write= rewrite (to write again)

Tick each box with a correct definition

rewrite write again	**unkind** not kind	**preschool** before school	**bicycle** one-wheeled vehicle
midnight in the middle of night 12:00	**dislike** like very much	**unsolved** not solved	**improper** perfect
non-stop without stopping	**overeat** eat too much	**subway** under a road	**replace** place something again
inactive not active	**exhale** breathe out	**invisible** clearly seen	**cooperate** work jointly

Prefixes

Fill in the blanks by adding a prefix to the words in brackets. Then write the number that matches the meaning of the word.

1. Abbie loves to do pottery. She always ____________ (plans) her projects.
2. She does not like ________ (order).
3. First she __________ her tools (arranges).
4. Then Abbie brings in an __________ lump of clay (formed).
5. She slowly ______________ the lump (shapes).
6. Abbie is ________ to see that the lump doesn't take a proper shape (happy).
7. She _______ upon her idea (thinks).
8. She __________ the project and moves the wheel carefully this time (starts).
9. The lump __________ and comes to shape a big pot! (appears)
10. Abbie paints the pot and puts it on a ________ (view).

____ opposite of appears	____shapes again	___sad	___think again
___plan before	__ not formed	____ not in order	___ show in advance
	___start again	___ arrange before	

Suffixes

Complete the sentences by adding a suffix to the words in bold.

A suffix is a word that is added at the end of a word to change the meaning of that word.

1. Some **play**______ sheep broke Mr Franc's fence.
2. He wonders if the fence is **use**__________.
3. Mr Franc thinks whether the fence is **repair**____________.
4. He looks **sad**__________ at the fence.
5. He **immediate** ____________ calls his friend Mr John.
6. Mr John is a **skil** ____________ handyman.
7. He repairs fences and gates **fast**__________ than other handymen.
8. He comes to Mr Franc's farm with all his **equip**__________.
9. Mr John works in the **bright**_________ of the day.
10. Mr Franc is full of **excite** _________ to see the new fence.

Hints -ful -ly -ment -able -er -ness

Suffixes

Complete each sentence by adding a suffix to the base word.

1. Toby and Abby took a rest_______ night's sleep before hiking.
2. They packed their backpacks and did not carry anything break________.
3. Abby wore comfort________ shoes.
4. Toby's shoes are sturdy and wear________.
5. The children also carry a jacket in case the day is cold and wind______.
6. The group was full of excite___________.
7. Toby was the lead____ of the group.
8. He told the group not to litter and keep the trails spot___________.
9. The children are thought________ and help each other while hiking.
10. They speak softly because loud_________ sounds can scare animals.
11. Everyone was happy to see colour______ flowers and animals.
12. The trip was memor____________ for the children.

Using Suffixes

Fill in the crossword by adding a suffix to the words in the word bank. Read the hints for changing spellings.

Across

3. state of being dense
6. full of courage
8. one who is slow than the other
10. the act of celebrating

Down

1. a person who makes art
2. without fear
4. state of being perfect
5. something that can be solved
7. something that can be read
9. full of help

Quick tip!

We add or remove letters while adding suffixes to some words. For example: to add –ion to celebrate, drop the e at the end and add –ion. The new word is celebration.

-ion or –tion: action or process
-ity: state of being
-ment: action or process
-able: can be done
-less: without
-ous: full of
-er: more

Greek Roots

We use some Greek roots to form new words in English. Read the list of some Greek roots in the table given below.

TRY IT

Use any 5 Greek roots and make 3 words for each.

Greek Root	Meaning	Greek Root	Meaning
aero	air	meter	measure
anthr	main	mono	one
ast	star	onym	name
biblio	book	opt	eye
bio	life	ortho	straight
cardi	heart	path	feeling
chrom	colour	phil	love
chron	time	phob	fear
cycl	circle	phon	sound
derm	skin	photo	light
geo	earth	phys	nature
gon	angle	phyte	plant
graph	write	pod	foot
hydr	water	scop	see
log	word	therm	heat

Greek Roots

Circle the Greek roots in each word below. Then write the letter of its meaning on the blank.

a. telephone	d. phonics	g. monogram
b. autograph	e. hemisphere	h. hydrosphere
c. bicycle	f. biology	i. thermometer

Now use the roots from the above words to complete these words.

1. ________ ical	4. ________ mobile	7. ________ lone
2. ________ al	5. ________ sphere	8. ________ ant
3. ________ scope	6. sym________ ny	9. ________ logue

word bank

_____ far
_____ sound
_____ water
_____ half
_____ one
_____ two
_____ life
_____ heat
_____ by itself

Compound Words

A compound word is a word made of two or more words used together.
For example: shoe + lace= shoelace

Read each word below. Combine it with a word from the help box and form a compound word.

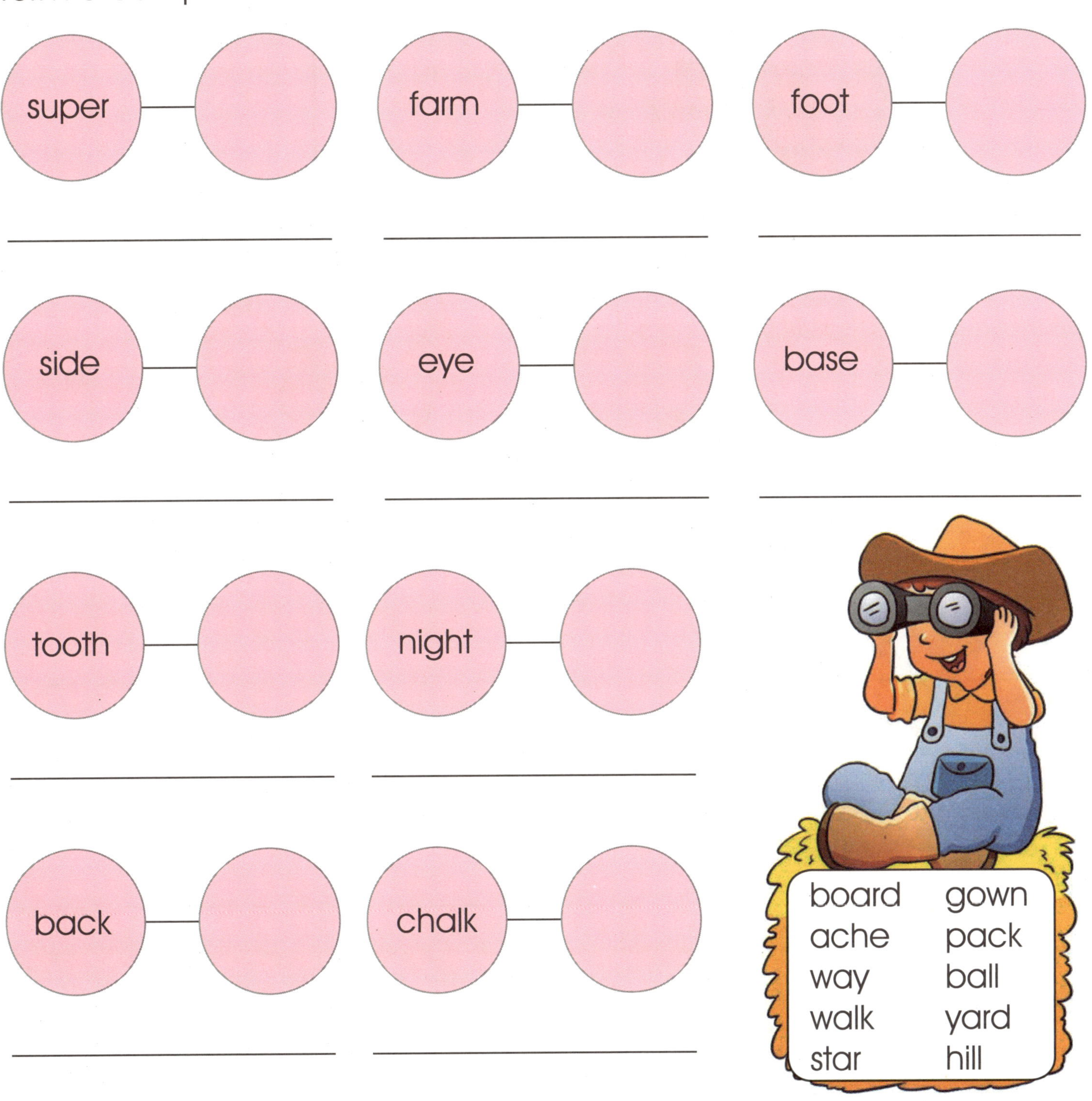

Compound Words

Write compound words using the help box given here.

1. ____________________

2. ____________________

3. ____________________

4. ____________________

5. ____________________

6. ____________________

7. ____________________

8. ____________________

9. ____________________

10. ____________________

11. ____________________

12. ____________________

TRY IT

Add ship, board and ball to words of your choice and make compound words.

Using Compound Words In Context

Draw lines to make compound words. Use the new words in the sentences given below.

1. ______________ is a nice winter day.
2. The __________ is bright and warm.
3. John slides down the ______________ past the car.
4. He turns around at the _______________.
5. He and his sister Olive play in the snow and make ___________.
6. Olive wants to make a _____________ too.
7. John runs into the house to get ___________ he collected last summer.
8. They make a big snowman and decorate it with the ___________ John brought.

sun	man
to	shells
snow	shine
side	way
drive	balls
snow	thing
some	day
sea	walk

TRY IT

Make three compound words using the words given below.
These words name furry decorations.
coat, ear, ring, pony, rain, tail

Using Compound Words

Circle the pair of words that make a compound words. Then fill in the blanks using an appropriate compound word.

break	way	through	fast
pan	cakes	walk	over
door	knob	bell	side
sun	ray	due	shine
door	knob	way	bell
table	cloth	land	chair
tea	pot	berry	spoon
sun	bun	back	flowers

Nora was preparing__________. Just as she began heating up the frying pan for __________, the __________ rang. She took the frying pan off the stove and went to answer the door. As she opened the door, __________ spilled in through the __________.

"Welcome I'm glad you could come by for breakfast. Come in and have a seat, Abby." she said.

Nora spread a __________ on the table and set out her crystal __________ beside the vase of __________.

Nora and Abby sat down and had a delicious breakfast together.

Contractions

A contraction is a short form of a word or words. These are formed by replacing missing letters with an apostrophe.

For example: he will – he'll

Use the words on each gift to make contractions. Write them on the blanks.

1. ____________________
2. ____________________
3. ____________________
4. ____________________
5. ____________________
6. ____________________
7. ____________________
8. ____________________
9. ____________________
10. ____________________

Contractions

Read the sentences.
Replace the underlined words by a contraction.

1. <u>It is</u> Christmas today.
2. <u>We are</u> looking for Martha's present.
3. <u>Where is</u> the present kept?
4. Jacob thinks <u>it is</u> behind the wardrobe.
5. <u>I am</u> going to look for the present in the living room.
6. Tina <u>does not</u> remember seeing Martha's present.
7. Jacob and Martha also said they <u>had not</u> seen her present.
8. <u>They have</u> been searching all around the house.
9. <u>I will</u> look for the present in the garage.
10. Martha <u>cannot</u> wait until the celebration begins.

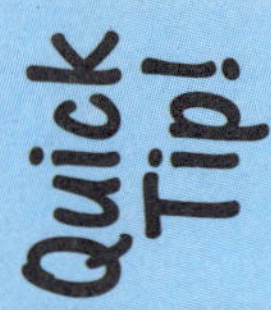

We use **'s** to show contractions and possessive nouns.

It's is the contraction of **It is. Martha's** means something that belongs to Martha.

Contractions

Fill in the blanks with suitable contractions from the given options and read the sentences..

1. Poor Maria ______________ invited to the party.
2. Her friends are invited. They ____________ wait to go there.
3. ___________ been planning for it all day.
4. Maria ___________ feel happy about it.
5. She __________ have a nice dress to wear at the party
6. Maria's sister ___________ allow her to go anyway.
7. __________ stay at home by herself.
8. Maria thinks ____________ unfair that she has not been invited.
9. But ___________ a surprise waiting for her!
10. Her friends ___________ believe it when they see the surprise.

Fun With Words

Here's a crazy z puzzle! Add letter z to each word below. You can add the letter in the beginning, middle or at the end. Then rearrange the words to make a new word.

Example:
one+ z = zone

1. spa + z = ________
2. ill + z = ________
3. bear + z = ________
4. are + z = ________
5. ero + z = ________
6. ame + z = ________
7. doe + z = ________
8. moo + z = ________
9. ripe + z = ________
10. roar + z = ________
11. done + z = ________
12. noose + z = ________

TRY IT

What does an alarm do continuously to wake you up?

Hint: It has a z in it!

Silent Letters

Silent letters are letters of a word that you can't hear when you say it.
Example: knew is pronounced as new as the k is silent.

Identify the silent letter or letters in each word below and circle it.

TRY IT

Say this tongue-twister 5 times quickly and identify the words that have a silent letter?

John Johnson joined Jenny Jerry in eating whole apple jelly.

Silent Letters

Unscramble the letters to complete each sentence with silent-letter words.

1. Suzie's holidays are _______________ (htrig) around the corner.
2. She has only ___________ (ghtie) days left for shopping.
3. Suzie _______________(houtght) about all that she wants to buy.
4. She and her mother _____________(rwote) a list.
5. They went shopping an ___________(uhro) later.
6. Suzie _____________(ghtbou) a cap for her sister.
7. She bought a warm _____________(niktedt) scarf for her mother.
8. She _____________(rawppde) her presents nicely.

TRY IT

Write 3 words each with silent k and w. Circle the silent letters.

Word Choices

Word choice refers to the selection of words to make your writing interesting.
Example: I heard a mew and went into the room.
I heard a mew and rushed into the room.

Choose the best word for each sentence given below.

1. James ______________ his swimsuit out of the drawer.
   a. got | b. yanked

2. He ____________ his swim tube from under the bed.
   a. looked | b. spotted

3. James ____________ on his water goggles.
   a. grabbed | b. put

4. Then he ______________ out of the room.
   a. went | b. dashed

5. The pool water was _______________ with chlorine.
   a. cleaned | b. disinfected

6. James _______________ into the pool and enjoyed himself.
   a. jumped | b. splashed

7. It was a _____________ day for swimming.
   a. better | b. perfect

Word Skills

Use the codes below to write the opposite of each word.

1. always

___ ___ ___ ___ ___

8 % / % *

2. strong

___ ___ ___ ___

= % @ 5

3. sweet

___ ___ ___ ___

& 9) *

4. shallow

___ ___ ___ ___

& % % ?

5. idle

___ ___ ___ ___

) & :

6. agree

___ ___ ___ ___ ___ ___ ___ ___

& 3 & @ 1 * % %

7. rare

___ ___ ___ ___ ___ ___

$ 9 7 7 9 8

8. rapid

___ ___ ___ ___

& 6 9 =

9. full

___ ___ ___ ___ ___

% 7 ? (:

10. danger

___ ___ ___ ___

& @ > %

code

a- @	b- #	c- $
d- &	e- %	f- >
g- 1	h- 2	i- 3
j- 4	k- 5	l- 6
m- 7	n- 8	o- 9
p- ?	q- +	r- *
s- &	t- (	u-)
v- /	w- =	x- <
y- :	z- [	

Words Often Confused

Choose the correct options and complete the sentences. Find the words in the puzzle.

N	O	X	M	H	R	Y	R	L	B
P	U	Y	F	A	I	R	I	I	Y
I	U	T	H	E	R	E	G	M	V
E	A	R	B	A	D	N	H	K	I
C	T	H	E	R	E	H	T	U	C
E	D	C	L	W	V	M	E	N	R
S	D	L	C	X	A	I	S	H	Z
N	Q	U	R	E	V	U	O	Z	P
X	S	W	E	A	R	Q	A	P	P
G	Y	B	U	Y	W	H	R	U	E

1. Would you please bring the coat ___________(hear, here)?
2. The children are going to the ___________ (fair, fare).
3. Ken uses his ___________ (write, right) hand to draw.
4. _____________(Their, There) are some cookies in the jar.
5. Linda will _____________ (wear, where) a long dress for the party.
6. The kites _____________(sore, soar) high in the sky.
7. Kate will ___________(buy, by) a new watch next month.
8. Maria cut the cake into eight equal __________(peaces, pieces)

Using Context Clues

Read the text.
Write the words in bold next to their meanings.

TRY IT

Use any three of the words in bold in sentences of your own.

Puzzle Time!

Listed below are meanings of some words. Read the meaning and look out for the word.
Then complete the words by writing the missing letters.

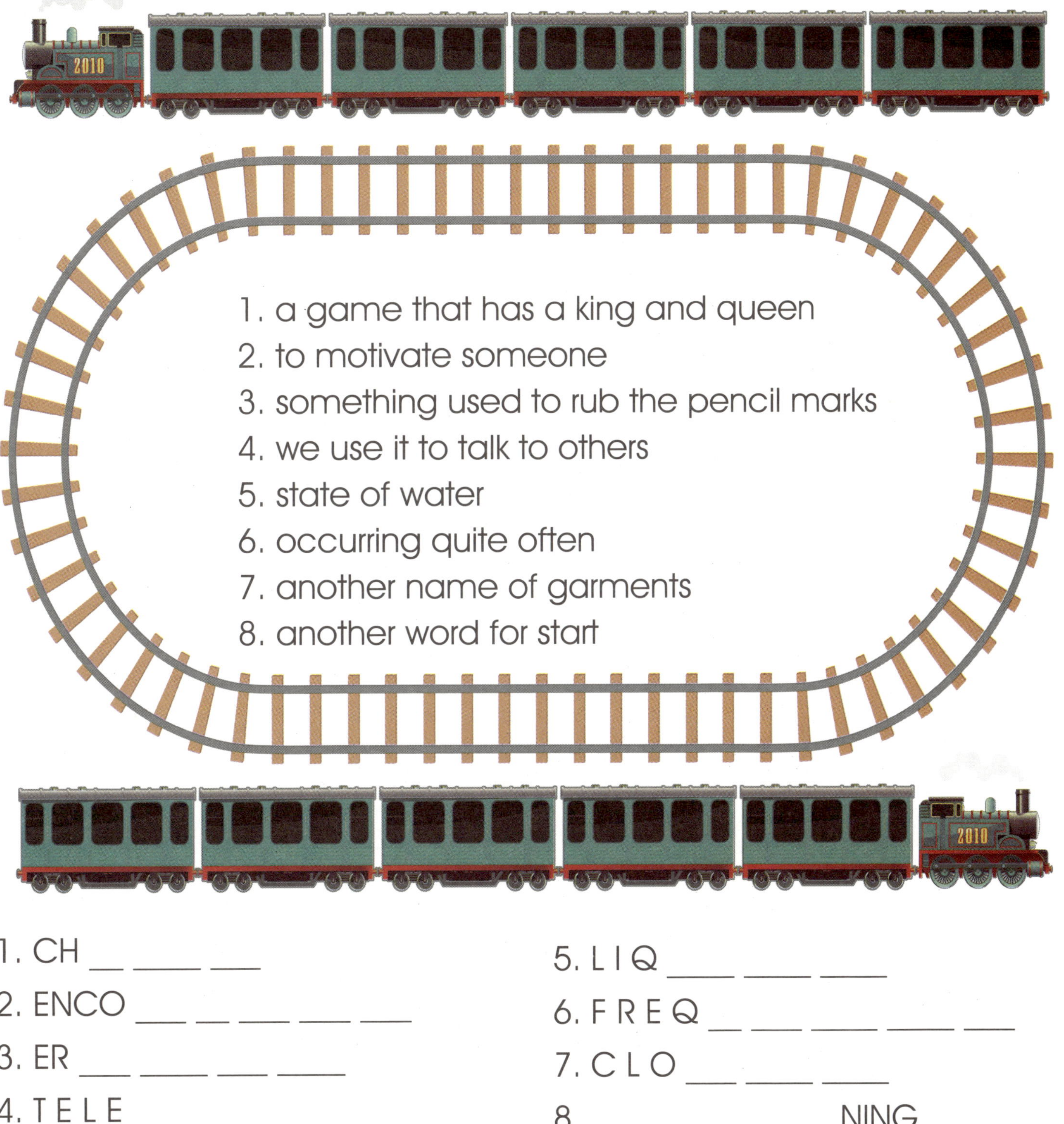

1. CH ___ ___ ___
2. ENCO ___ ___ ___ ___ ___
3. ER ___ ___ ___ ___
4. T E L E ___ ___ ___ ___ ___ ___
5. L I Q ___ ___ ___
6. F R E Q ___ ___ ___ ___ ___
7. C L O ___ ___ ___
8. ___ ___ ___ ___ ___ NING

Answer Key

Page 2

Children will do on their own.
Answers will vary

Page 3

1. rats
2. evil, live
3. draw
4. kids
5. cafe
6. plug
7. sore

puzzle answer: Eight ate

Page 4

school

read

leaf

run

sheep

swift

kite

master

happy

Page 5

1. play
2. enjoy
3. nice
4. love
5. end
6. try
7. build
8. cold
9. heat
10. sleep

Page 6

1. dived
2. carried
3. talked
4. washed
5. skipped
6. tried
7. planned
8. jogged
9. hurried
10. hopped

Page 7

Children will do on their own.

Page 8

rewrite √ write again	**unkind** √ not kind	**preschool** √ before school	**bicycle** one-wheeled vehicle
midnight √ in the middle of night 12:00	**dislike** like very much	**unsolved** √ not solved	**improper** perfect
nonstop √ without stopping	**overeat** √ eat too much	**subway** √ under a road	**replace** place something again
inactive √ not active	**exhale** √ breathe out	**invisible** clearly seen	**cooperate** √ work jointly

Page 9

1. preplans
2. disorder
3. prearranges
4. unformed
5. reshapes
6. unhappy
7. rethinks
8. restarts
9. disappears
10. preview

Page 10

1. playful
2. useful
3. repairable
4. sadly
5. immediately
6. skilful
7. faster
8. equipment
9. brightness
10. excitement

Page 11

1. restful
2. breakable
3. comfortable
4. wearable
5. windy
6. excitement
7. leader
8. spotless
9. thoughtful
10. louder
11. colourful
12. memorable

Answer Key

Page 12

Across

3. state of being dense

6. full of courage

8. one who is slow than the other

10. the act of celebrating

Down

1. a person who makes art

2. without fear

4. state of being perfect

5. something that can be solved

7. something that can be read

9. full of help

Page 14

a. tele

b. auto

c. cycl

d. phon

e. spher

f. bio

g. mono

h. hydro

i. therm

1. spherical
2. thermal
3. telescope
4. automobile
5. biosphere
6. symphony
7. cyclone
8. hydrant
9. monologue

Page 15

superstar

farmyard

foothill

sidewalk

eyeball

baseball

toothache

nightgown

backpack

chalkboard

Page 16

teamwork

sunset

homesick

flagpole

windshield

drumstick

scorekeeper

myself

downtown

racetrack

homework

flagstick

Page 17

1. today
2. sunshine
3. sidewalk
4. driveway
5. snowballs
6. snowman
7. something
8. seashells

Page 18

breakfast

pancakes

doorbell

sunshine

doorway

tablecloth

teapot

sunflowers

Page 19

1. he's
2. who'll
3. I'm
4. haven't
5. you're
6. she'd
7. they'd
8. don't
9. let's
10. there's

Page 20

1. It's
2. We're
3. Where's
4. It's
5. I'm
6. doesn't
7. hadn't
8. They've
9. I'll
10. can't

Answer Key

Page 21

1. isn't
2. can't
3. they're
4. didn't
5. doesn't
6. won't
7. she'll
8. it's
9. there's
10. wouldn't

Page 22

1. zaps
2. zill
3. zebra
4. raze
5. zero
6. maze
7. doze
8. zoom
9. prize
10. razor
11. dozen
12. snooze

Page 23

1. l
2. h
3. k
4. l
5. l
6. k
7. g
8. b
9. h
10. b

Page 24

1. right
2. eight
3. thought
4. wrote
5. hour
6. bought
7. knitted
8. wrapped

Page 25

1. yanked
2. spotted
3. grabbed
4. dashed
5. disinfected
6. splashed
7. perfect

Page 26

1. never
2. weak
3. sour
4. deep
5. busy
6. disagree
7. common
8. slow
9. empty
10. safe

Page 27

1. here
2. fair
3. right
4. There
5. wear
6. soar
7. buy
8. pieces

Page 28

1. require- need
2. normally- usually
3. thought- wondered
4. take care of- nurture
5. land covered in thick grass- grasslands
6. the natural home- habitats
7. moist- humid
8. grow well- thrive

Page 29

1. CHESS
2. ENCOURAGE
3. ERASER
4. TELEPHONE
5. LIQUID
6. FREQUENT
7. CLOTHES
8. BEGINNING